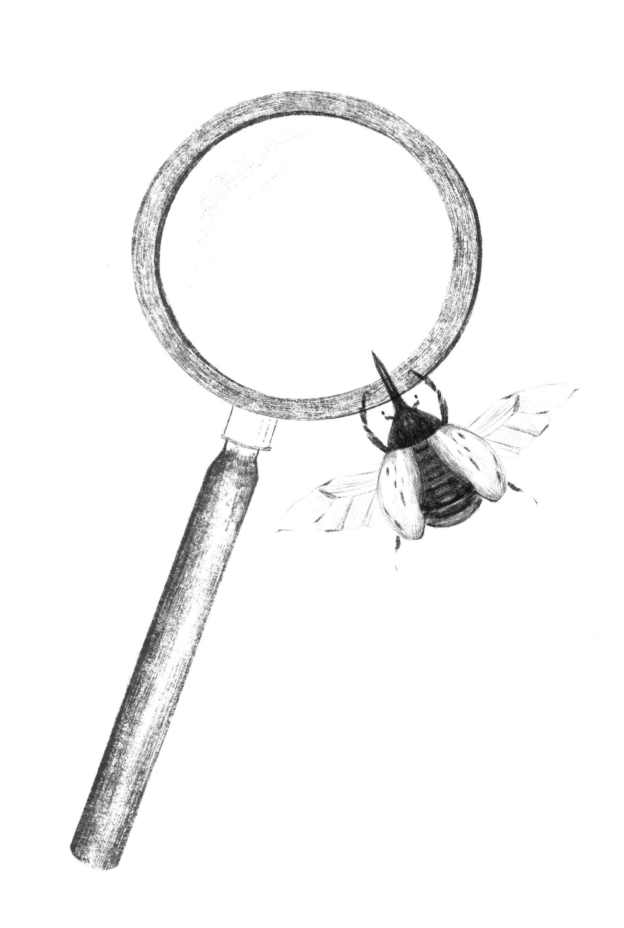

CONTENTS

CHAN'S MEGASTICK – 57CM LONG (22.4 INCHES)

Just imagine meeting an ant more than six and a half feet long. It would probably be more terrifying than a lion or a tiger, wouldn't it? The ant's jaws would be over three feet long and it would be able to bite through a table leg and run faster than a leopard. Think about this next time you see an ant and it won't just look like a simple little insect.

Scientists have calculated how many ants live on our planet and the number has lots and lots of zeroes: millions of billions.

Yet, ants are only a tiny part of the world of insects.

Scientists have already discovered more than one million different species of insects and each of these includes millions, or even billions, of creatures. Every day, all over the world, these insects go about their lives in many different ways. Many can fly; others walk, or burrow into wood. Some we find beautiful, like butterflies, others we find much less appealing, such as cockroaches. Some insects are unusually large and we can see them very clearly. . . they are almost scary! But most insects are small and some are so tiny that we need a magnifying glass to see them. When you find them here, in the pages of this book, you will see them in their life-size version as well as in magnified drawings that will show you all of their extraordinary details.

HARLEQUIN BEETLE
7.5CM LONG (3 INCHES)

If there were no insects, the world would be very different and, perhaps, there would be no life on Earth, at least not as we know it. Without the insects, many flowers would disappear. Countless animals like birds, lizards and bats would no longer exist. Many living beings depend on insects for their survival, including human beings.

In this book, you will see life-size insects, large and small, you will find out how much they weigh, how fast they are and how many of them there are. Maybe you will no longer feel frightened of the biggest ones with the strangest appearances. Maybe you will even begin to find them fascinating. After all, they are some of our oldest friends in Nature.

LITTLE BARRIER ISLAND GIANT WETA - 8.5CM LONG (3.3 INCHES)

HOW MANY INSECTS CAN YOU SEE?

Insects from all over the world have gathered on this page. Of course, you will never see such a variety together in a field or a wood near home.
Can you see all the insects in this drawing?
On the next page, you can check how many you found.
You will discover their names and where they live.

PUSS MOTH CATERPILLAR
8CM LONG (3.1 INCHES)
EUROPE AND ASIA

DEATH'S-HEAD HAWKMOTH
12CM LONG (4.7 INCHES)
EUROPE, ASIA AND AFRICA

PUSS MOTH
WINGSPAN 7CM (2.7 INCHES)
EUROPE AND ASIA

VERDANT HAWK
WINGSPAN 11CM
(4.3 INCHES)
AFRICA

QUEEN ALEXANDRA'S BIRDWING
MALE: WINGSPAN 20CM (7.8 INCHES)
PAPUA NEW GUINEA

YOUNG OF THE PINK
ORCHID MANTIS
3.5CM LONG (1.3 INCHES)
INDONESIA

THERE ARE
8 INSECTS.
DID YOU FIND
THEM ALL?

DUNG BEETLE
ABOUT 3CM LONG
(1.1 INCHES)

NEST OF SOUTHERN
WOOD ANTS
0.9CM LONG (0.3 INCHES)
EUROPE

PERUVIAN GRASSHOPPER - WINGSPAN 18CM (7 INCHES)

An insect's body is very complex and with so many insects in existence, there is an endless variety of shapes and colors. Just think how different a ladybug and a butterfly are!
If we use a magnifying glass, we can see some of the details of their bodies that are difficult to see with the naked eye. They are very strange and interesting.

• A MIXED BAG OF INSECTS....

The rear wings of grasshoppers open out like a fan so that these insects can both jump and fly!

CUCKOO WASP - 0.7CM LONG (0.2 INCHES)

The cuckoo wasp lays its eggs in the nests of other wasps, just like the cuckoo, which lays its eggs in the nests of other birds.

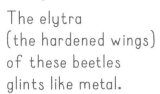

The elytra
(the hardened wings)
of these beetles
glints like metal.

The horsefly bites to
suck blood, like a mosquito,
but it is much bigger
and its eyes look like
colored glass.

DARK GIANT HORSEFLY - 3CM LONG (1.1 INCHES)

PAPER WASP - 1.5CM LONG (0.6 INCHES)

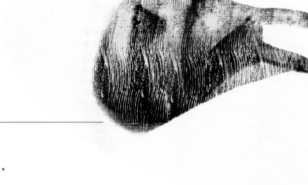

This is the wasp's
weapon, a long,
poisonous stinger...
it is a good idea to
leave it alone!

The hummingbird
hawk-moth usually
keeps its proboscis
rolled up, but when it
unrolls, it is very long
and it is used as a straw
to drink nectar from
the flowers.

HUMMINGBIRD HAWK-MOTH - WINGSPAN 4.5CM (1.7 INCHES)

Insects lay very small eggs; to see them you need a magnifying glass, or even better, a microscope. Some have strange and interesting shapes; they are very different from bird's eggs! Let's look at some of them.

ROYAL WALNUT MOTH

ORANGE TIP

GIANT STRONG-NOSED STINK BUG

* ON THE NEXT PAGE, YOU CAN SEE THE CATERPILLARS AND THE ADULTS.

MADAGASCAR MOON MOTH*

ADONIS BLUE

HARLEQUIN CABBAGE BUG

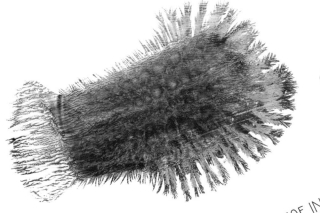

LEAF INSECT

ON PAGE 36, YOU CAN SEE AN ADULT LEAF INSECT.

Not all newborn insects look like their parents. When you look closely at a caterpillar, it is hard to imagine that it will become a butterfly: it must be magic! Not only butterflies change as they grow — beetles, flies, bees, ants and many other insects develop from un-recognizable larvae. On the other hand, some insects, like stink bugs, grasshoppers and stick insects look like miniature versions of their parents from the moment they are born.

The biggest and heaviest 'baby' insect is the larva of the Goliath Beetle that can weigh up to 100 grams (3.5 ounces)! It shelters underground, where it eats the roots of grass and when it comes out, its appearance has changed so much that it is hard to believe that it is the same creature!

GOLIATH BEETLE - 14CM LONG (5.5 INCHES), WEIGHT 100G (3.5OZ)

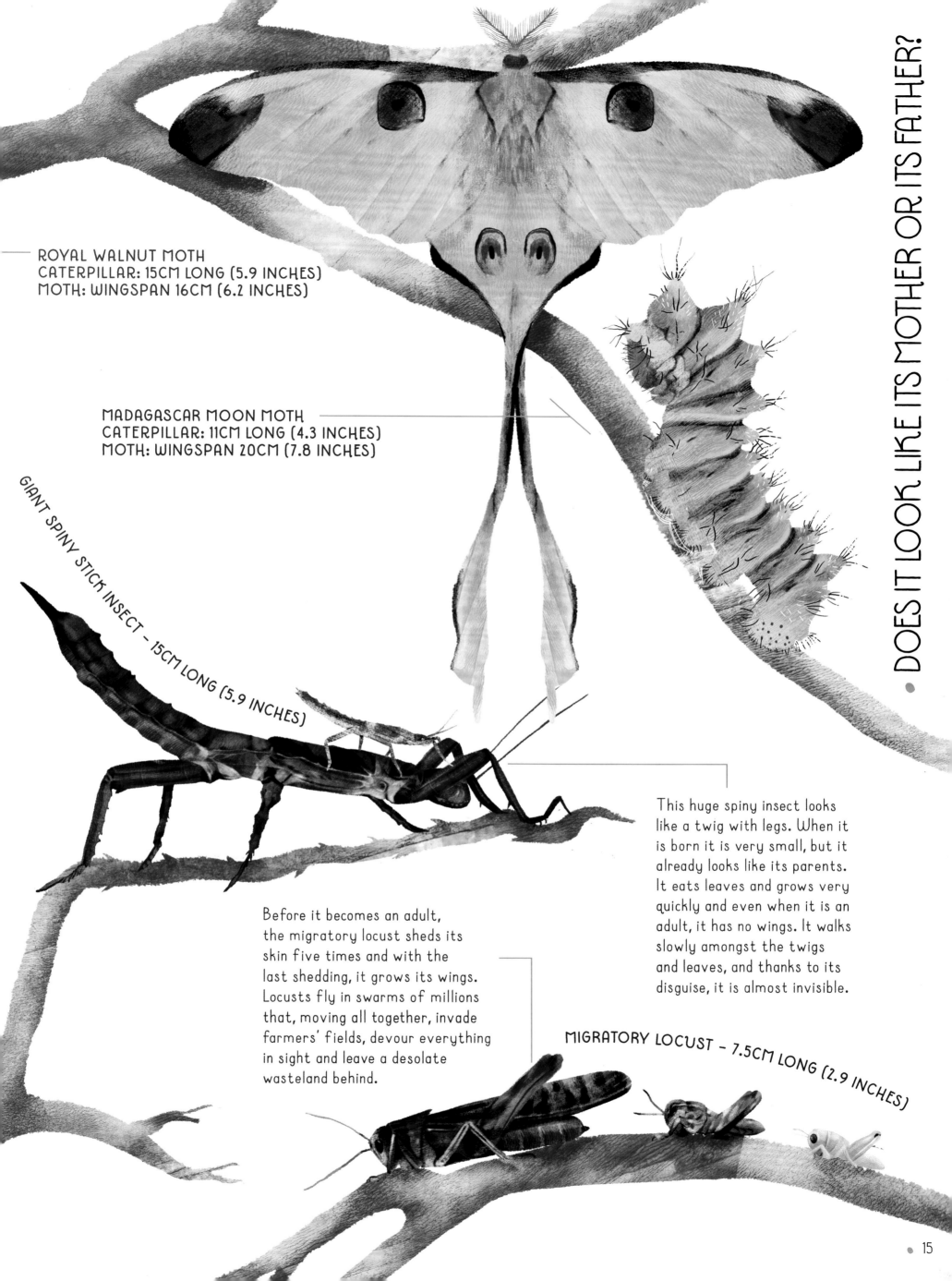

ROYAL WALNUT MOTH
CATERPILLAR: 15CM LONG (5.9 INCHES)
MOTH: WINGSPAN 16CM (6.2 INCHES)

MADAGASCAR MOON MOTH
CATERPILLAR: 11CM LONG (4.3 INCHES)
MOTH: WINGSPAN 20CM (7.8 INCHES)

GIANT SPINY STICK INSECT - 15CM LONG (5.9 INCHES)

This huge spiny insect looks like a twig with legs. When it is born it is very small, but it already looks like its parents. It eats leaves and grows very quickly and even when it is an adult, it has no wings. It walks slowly amongst the twigs and leaves, and thanks to its disguise, it is almost invisible.

Before it becomes an adult, the migratory locust sheds its skin five times and with the last shedding, it grows its wings. Locusts fly in swarms of millions that, moving all together, invade farmers' fields, devour everything in sight and leave a desolate wasteland behind.

MIGRATORY LOCUST - 7.5CM LONG (2.9 INCHES)

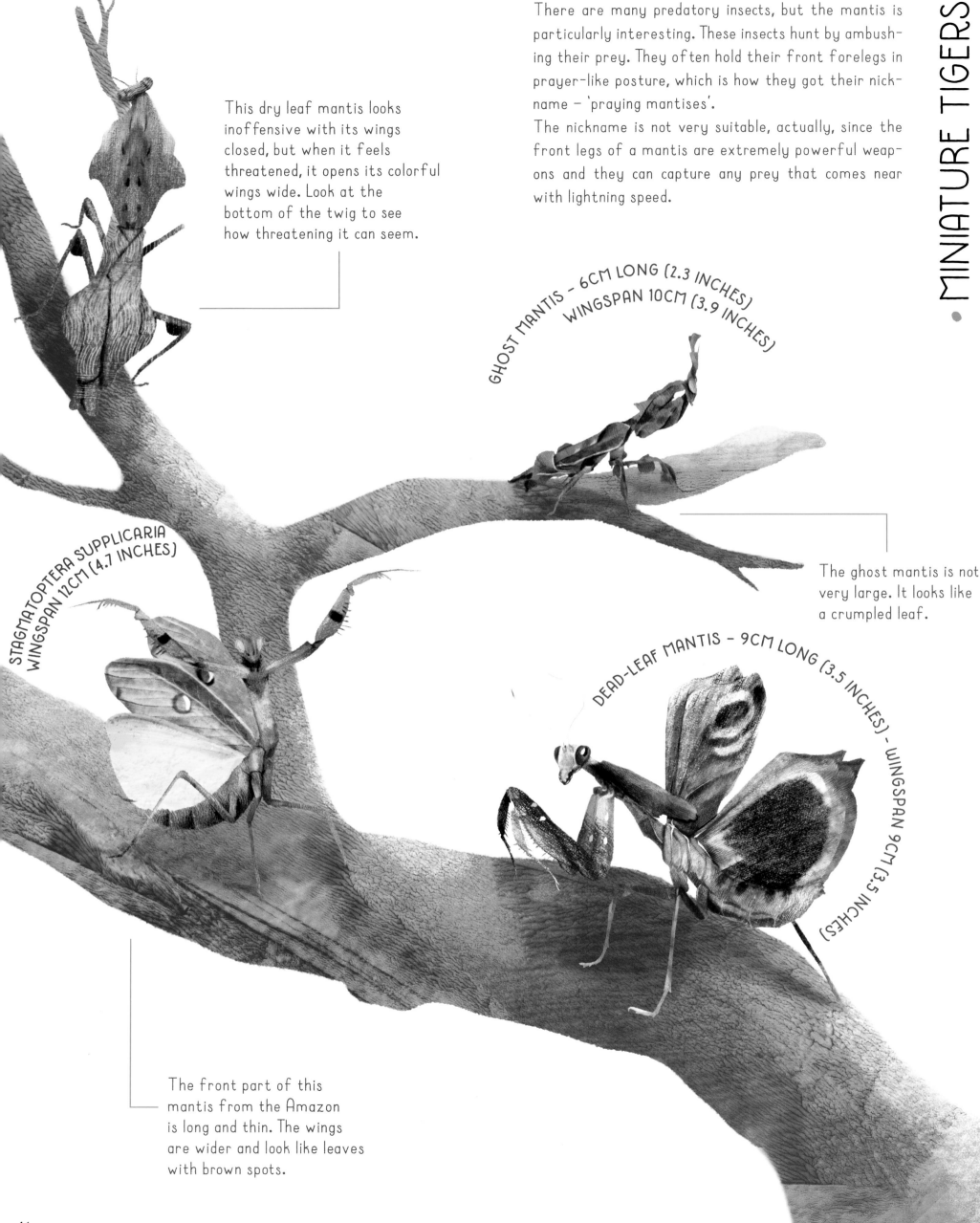

This dry leaf mantis looks inoffensive with its wings closed, but when it feels threatened, it opens its colorful wings wide. Look at the bottom of the twig to see how threatening it can seem.

There are many predatory insects, but the mantis is particularly interesting. These insects hunt by ambushing their prey. They often hold their front forelegs in prayer-like posture, which is how they got their nickname – 'praying mantises'.
The nickname is not very suitable, actually, since the front legs of a mantis are extremely powerful weapons and they can capture any prey that comes near with lightning speed.

GHOST MANTIS – 6CM LONG (2.3 INCHES) WINGSPAN 10CM (3.9 INCHES)

STAGMATOPTERA SUPPLICARIA WINGSPAN 12CM (4.7 INCHES)

The ghost mantis is not very large. It looks like a crumpled leaf.

DEAD-LEAF MANTIS – 9CM LONG (3.5 INCHES) – WINGSPAN 9CM (3.5 INCHES)

The front part of this mantis from the Amazon is long and thin. The wings are wider and look like leaves with brown spots.

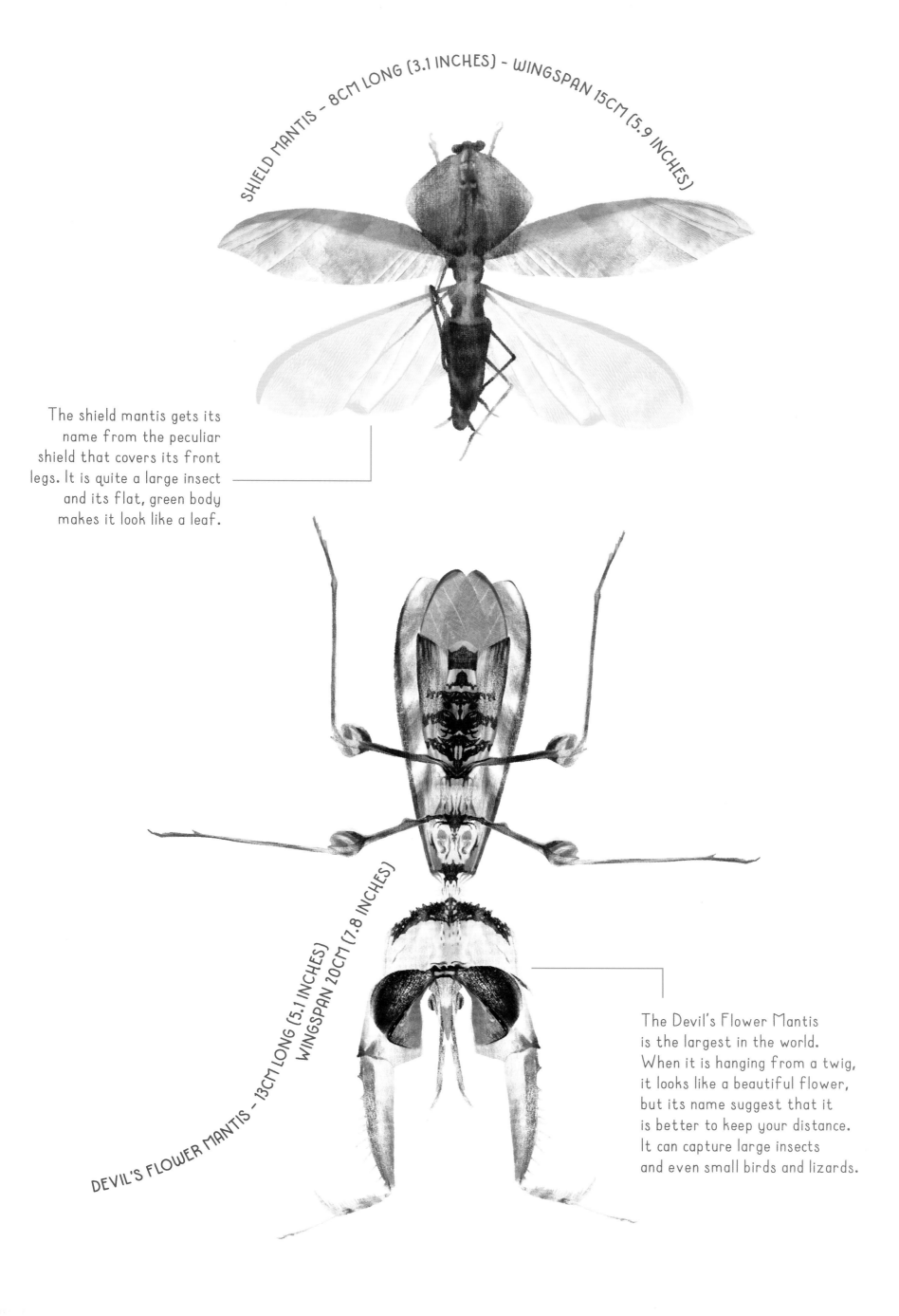

The shield mantis gets its name from the peculiar shield that covers its front legs. It is quite a large insect and its flat, green body makes it look like a leaf.

DEVIL'S FLOWER MANTIS - 13CM LONG (5.1 INCHES)
WINGSPAN 20CM (7.8 INCHES)

The Devil's Flower Mantis is the largest in the world. When it is hanging from a twig, it looks like a beautiful flower, but its name suggest that it is better to keep your distance. It can capture large insects and even small birds and lizards.

MONSTERS IN THE POND

Many insects can be found in the water of ponds and streams where they lay their eggs and live as larvae. Many, as adults, fly away but some, even though they can fly, stay here all their lives.

Dragonfly larvae, known as nymphs, live in water. Although they are quite small, they have something in common with their parents: they are fierce! Their mouths move forward to grasp their prey in sharp jaws.

NYMPH OF EMPEROR DRAGONFLY – 3CM LONG (1.1 INCHES)

GIANT WATER BUG – 4.5CM LONG (1.7 INCHES)

There are also fierce predators in a pond and the Broadest Diver is one of them. This large beetle swims very well and can even catch small fish and tadpoles.

GIANT WATER BUG LARVAE

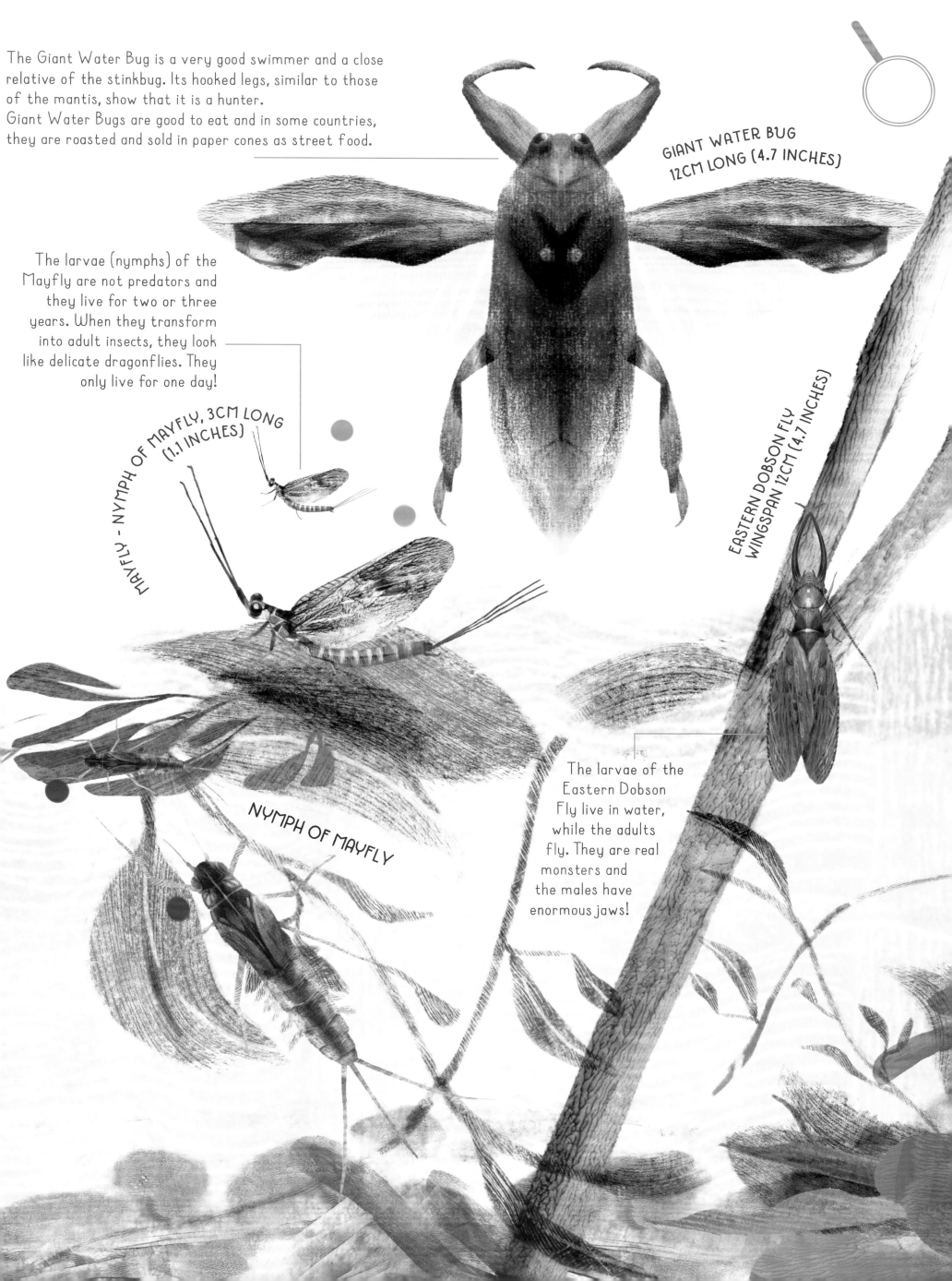

The Giant Water Bug is a very good swimmer and a close relative of the stinkbug. Its hooked legs, similar to those of the mantis, show that it is a hunter.
Giant Water Bugs are good to eat and in some countries, they are roasted and sold in paper cones as street food.

GIANT WATER BUG
12CM LONG (4.7 INCHES)

The larvae (nymphs) of the Mayfly are not predators and they live for two or three years. When they transform into adult insects, they look like delicate dragonflies. They only live for one day!

MAYFLY – NYMPH OF MAYFLY, 3CM LONG (1.1 INCHES)

EASTERN DOBSON FLY
WINGSPAN 12CM (4.7 INCHES)

NYMPH OF MAYFLY

The larvae of the Eastern Dobson Fly live in water, while the adults fly. They are real monsters and the males have enormous jaws!

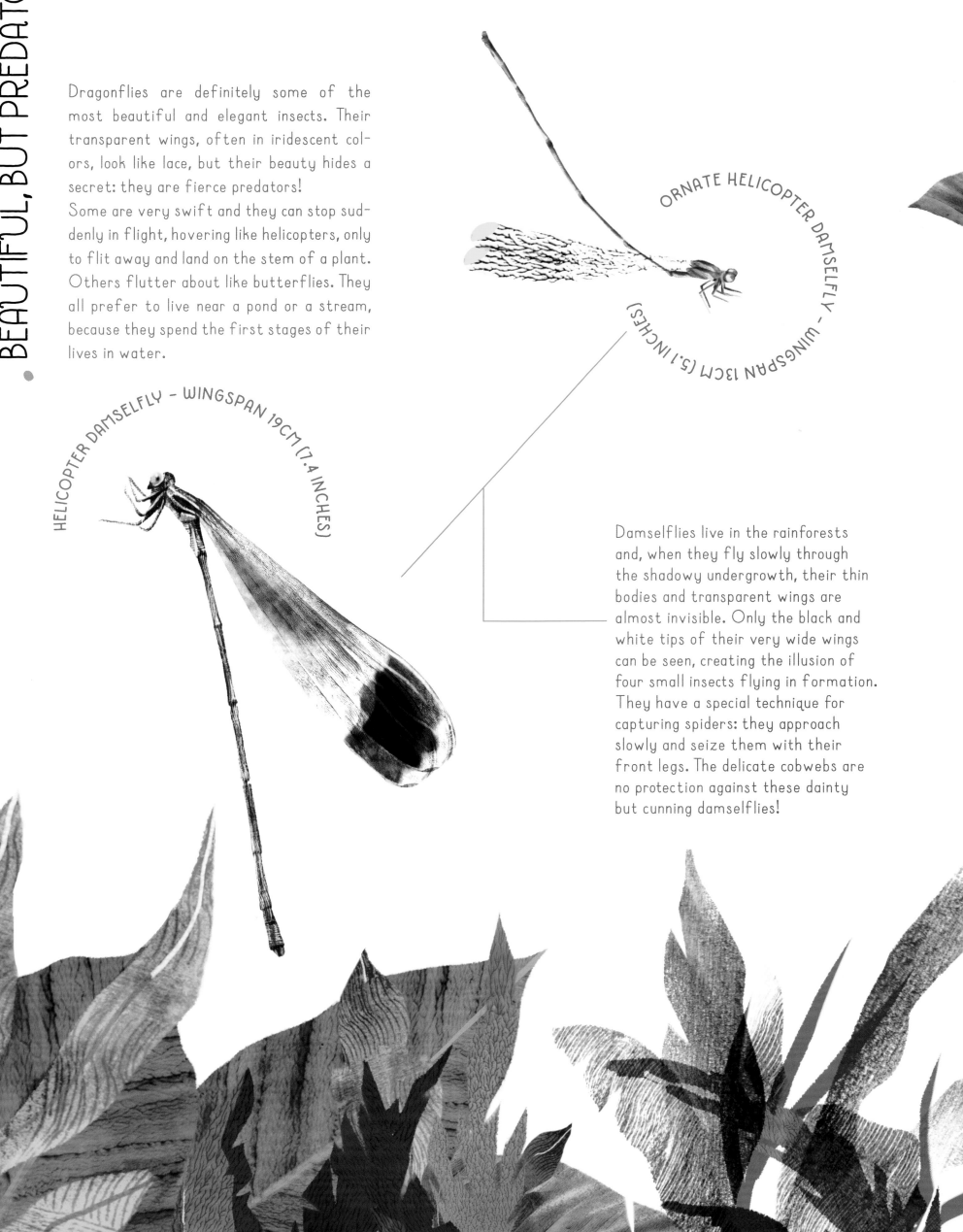

Dragonflies are definitely some of the most beautiful and elegant insects. Their transparent wings, often in iridescent colors, look like lace, but their beauty hides a secret: they are fierce predators!
Some are very swift and they can stop suddenly in flight, hovering like helicopters, only to flit away and land on the stem of a plant. Others flutter about like butterflies. They all prefer to live near a pond or a stream, because they spend the first stages of their lives in water.

ORNATE HELICOPTER DAMSELFLY - WINGSPAN 13CM (5.1 INCHES)

HELICOPTER DAMSELFLY - WINGSPAN 19CM (7.4 INCHES)

Damselflies live in the rainforests and, when they fly slowly through the shadowy undergrowth, their thin bodies and transparent wings are almost invisible. Only the black and white tips of their very wide wings can be seen, creating the illusion of four small insects flying in formation. They have a special technique for capturing spiders: they approach slowly and seize them with their front legs. The delicate cobwebs are no protection against these dainty but cunning damselflies!

GIANT PETALTAIL DRAGONFLY
WINGSPAN 15CM (5.9 INCHES)

BUSH DRAGONFLY
(KAPOKAPOWIA IN THE MAORI LANGUAGE)
WINGSPAN 13CM (5.1 INCHES)

EMPEROR DRAGONFLY
WINGSPAN 11CM (4.3 INCHES)

FOREST GIANT OWL – WINGSPAN 14CM (5.5 INCHES)

The eyes drawn on the wings of the Forest Giant Owl Butterfly look like those of a nocturnal bird of prey, a perfect trick for a peaceful life.

This caterpillar mimics a snake by swelling its head to look like a viper!

CATERPILLAR OF THE SPHINX MOTH – 11CM LONG (4.3 INCHES)

Insects have many preda-tors, like birds, lizards, frogs and small mammals, so many of them have found ways of scaring their enemies. Huge fake eyes on their wings give the impression that they be-long to a much bigger animal!

Some caterpillars have fake eyes that make them look like small and dangerous snakes. It is a very effective illusion!

CATERPILLAR OF THE SPICEBUSH SWALLOWTAIL

LANTERN FLY (PEANUT BUG) - LENGTH 9CM (3.5 INCHES) - WINGSPAN 15CM (5.9 INCHES)

The Lantern Fly is a relative of the cicadas. It has a strange elongated head, a bit like an alligator's, and when it spreads its wings, it displays two large eyes to scare away predators.

When this African Silk Moth is threatened, it spreads its wings to display two large, colorful eyes. If that is not enough to scare away the predator, it flaps its wings on the ground in a sort of skipping dance to create confusion.

AFRICAN SILK MOTH - WINGSPAN 18CM (7 INCHES)

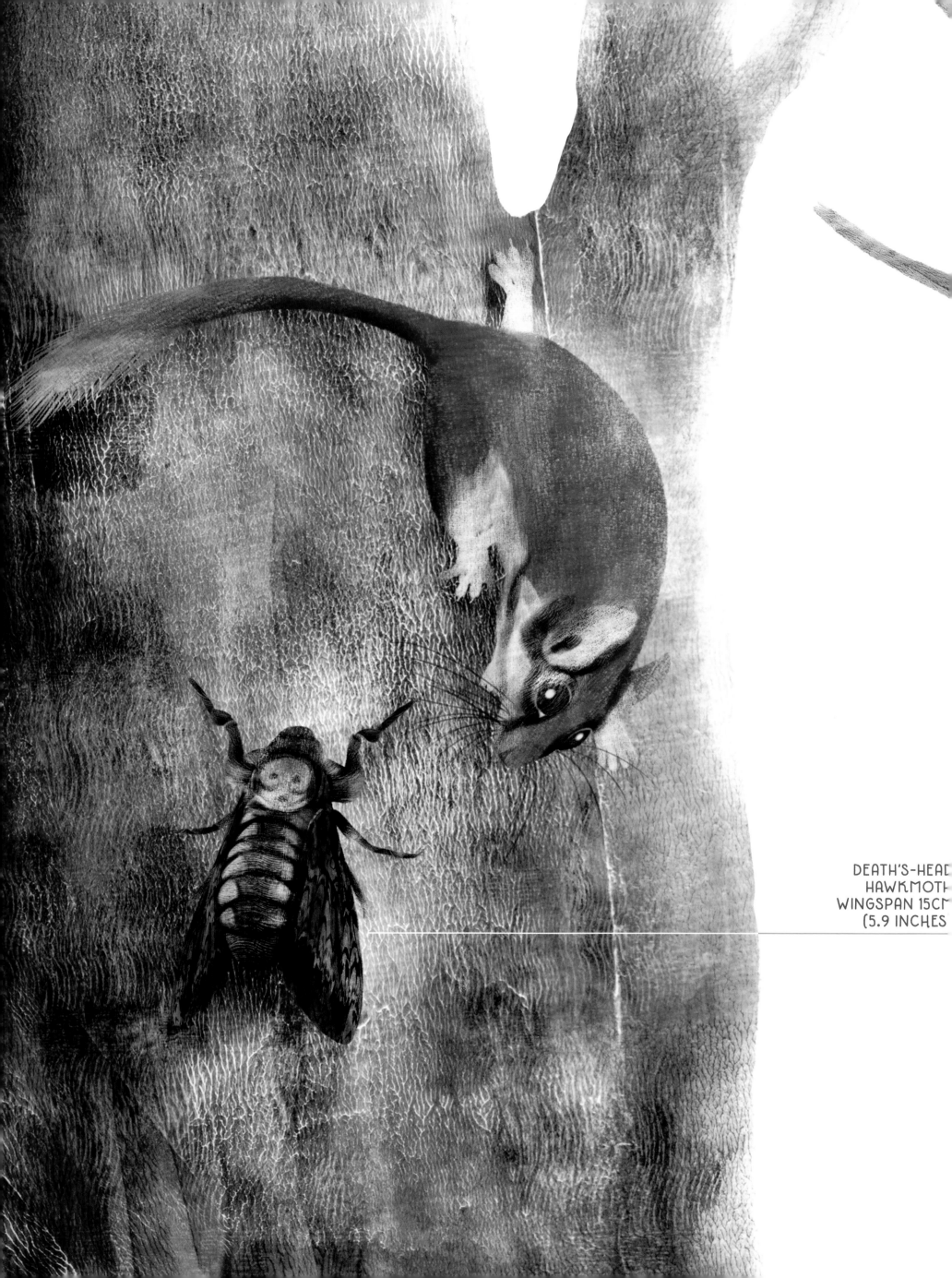

DEATH'S-HEAD
HAWKMOTH
WINGSPAN 15CM
(5.9 INCHES)

A TERRIFYING MOTH!

The Death's-head Hawkmoth is black and velvety and has a skull on its back, just like a pirate flag! Of course, it is only by chance that its markings resemble a skull and though it may look alarming to us, other animals take little notice of it. The moth has a different technique for scaring off predators — this is the only moth that can make noise and it screeches very loudly. This little dormouse was taken by surprise . . . better to find a less feisty prey!

The Death's-head Hawkmoth has another peculiar characteristic: instead of sucking nectar from the flowers, it flies into beehives and eats the bees' honey. Sometimes, it eats so much that it can't get out again and is killed by the bees.

HUMMINGBIRD HAWKMOTH
WINGSPAN 4.5CM (1.7 INCHES)

Here is another, much smaller, hawkmoth that hovers over flowers in the daytime; it is often mistaken for a hornet or even a hummingbird!

We know that the fruit of the oak tree is the acorn, so what are those odd shaped growths that we often see on their leaves? They are called galls. They are caused by the tiny Gall Wasps that lay their eggs in the buds of the tree and they are used to feed their larvae.

OAK GALL WASP

DOG ROSE GALL WASP

THEY ARE THERE, BUT WE CAN'T SEE THEM

There are many insects we can see and there are millions more all around us that we cannot see even when they are very close by. Let's all become detectives and try to track them down.

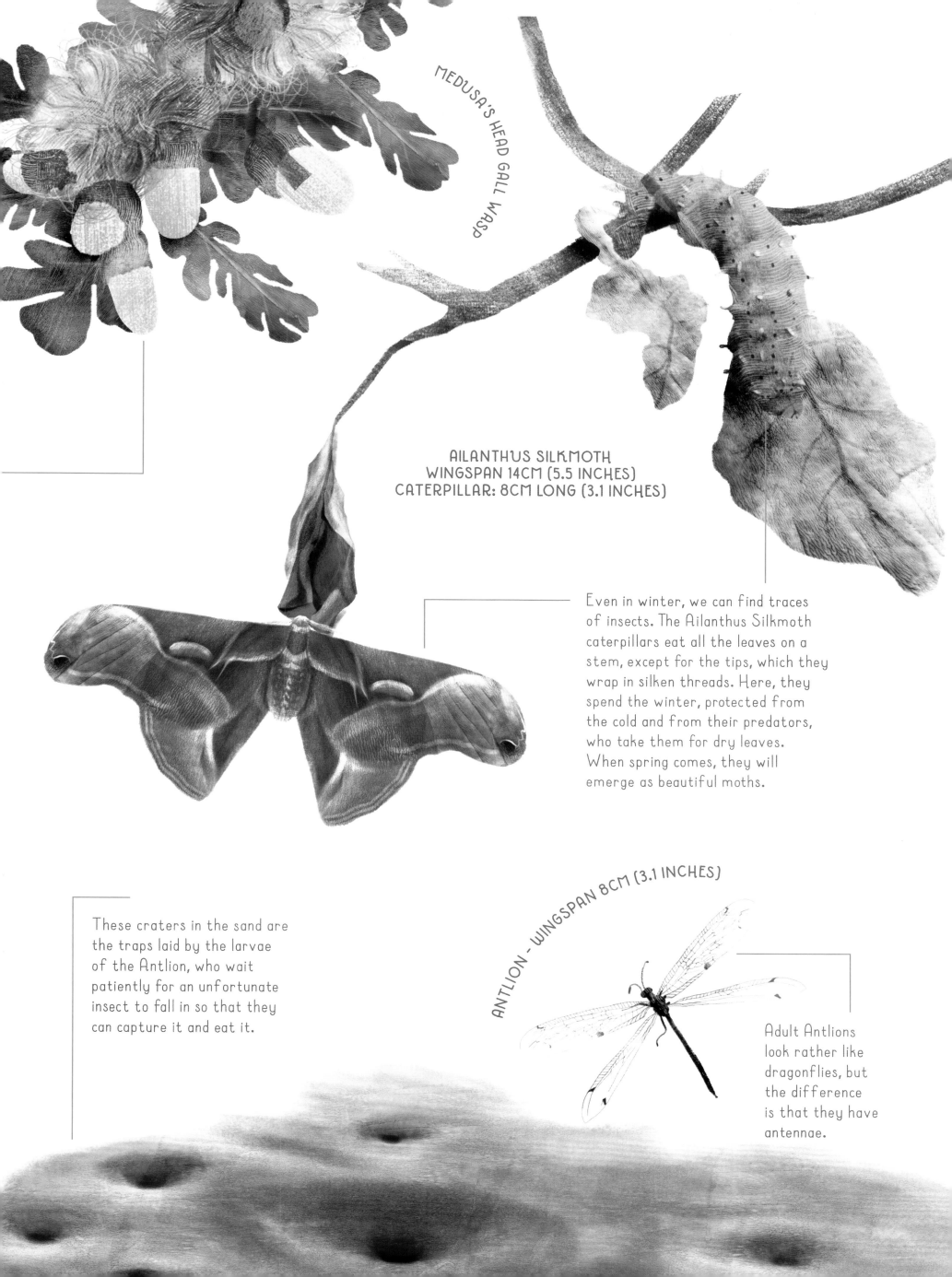

AILANTHUS SILKMOTH
WINGSPAN 14CM (5.5 INCHES)
CATERPILLAR: 8CM LONG (3.1 INCHES)

Even in winter, we can find traces of insects. The Ailanthus Silkmoth caterpillars eat all the leaves on a stem, except for the tips, which they wrap in silken threads. Here, they spend the winter, protected from the cold and from their predators, who take them for dry leaves. When spring comes, they will emerge as beautiful moths.

These craters in the sand are the traps laid by the larvae of the Antlion, who wait patiently for an unfortunate insect to fall in so that they can capture it and eat it.

ANTLION - WINGSPAN 8CM (3.1 INCHES)

Adult Antlions look rather like dragonflies, but the difference is that they have antennae.

AS SMALL AS AN ANT

Ants are common all over the world. Even though they are famous for their industriousness and their small size, there are many that are not small at all and some, that rather than industrious, should be described as pint-sized warriors.

GIANT KILLER ANT - FEMALE: 4CM LONG (1.5 INCHES) - MALE: 2.5CM LONG (0.9 INCHES)

These giant ants from the Amazon cannot compete with the huge beetles, but they are certainly impressive. They not only have large jaws, they can also give painful stings. Not exactly a harmless little ant...

LEAF-CUTTER ANT - 1.4CM LONG (0.5 INCHES)

Leaf-Cutter Ants do not eat leaves. They take them to their vast underground nests where they use them to make compost for growing the fungi they live on. They are clever little farmers!

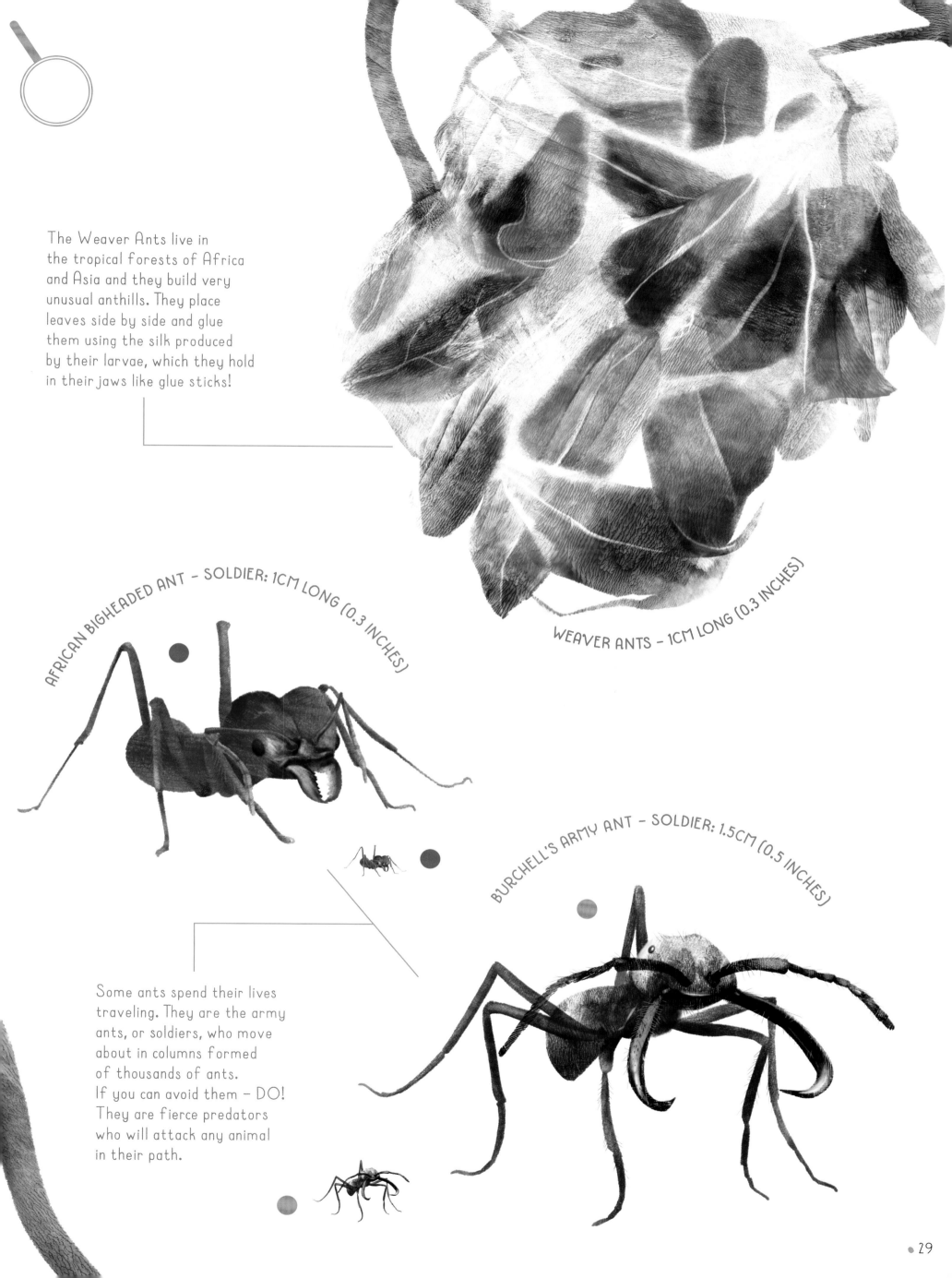

The Weaver Ants live in the tropical forests of Africa and Asia and they build very unusual anthills. They place leaves side by side and glue them using the silk produced by their larvae, which they hold in their jaws like glue sticks!

WEAVER ANTS – 1CM LONG (0.3 INCHES)

AFRICAN BIGHEADED ANT – SOLDIER: 1CM LONG (0.3 INCHES)

BURCHELL'S ARMY ANT – SOLDIER: 1.5CM (0.5 INCHES)

Some ants spend their lives traveling. They are the army ants, or soldiers, who move about in columns formed of thousands of ants. If you can avoid them – DO! They are fierce predators who will attack any animal in their path.

LIVING LIGHTS

On warm nights in late spring, fireflies (who are not actually flies, but beetles) flit about, transforming a simple meadow into an enchanted landscape. The males light up as they fly, while the females remain hidden in the grass and respond to the luminous invitations of their male counterparts with flashes of their own that differ according to the species.

FEMALE FIREFLY – 2.5CM LONG (1 INCH)

MALE PORTUGUESE FIREFLY – 1CM LONG (0.3 INCHES)

HEADLIGHT ELATOR
4.5CM LONG (1.7INCHES)

This beetle holds the record as the brightest insect in the world. With two luminous dots on its back and a luminous area on the abdomen, it emits a continuous, intense light. In some areas of the tropical forests in Central and South America, the local people use it as a living torch.

Thousands of tropical fireflies gather in a tree and light up the foliage by synchronizing their intermittent lights, just like the lights on a Christmas tree.

OWL MOTH - WINGSPAN 14CM (5.5 INCHES)

GIANT LEAF INSECT - 10CM LONG (3.9 INCHES)

During the day, moths keep very still, trying not to be noticed. The Owl Moth is very large, but when it settles on the trunk of a tree, it becomes invisible.

This is the largest of all of the grasshoppers that look like leaves. It has wings but it only uses them to camouflage itself in the foliage.

GIANT MALAYSIAN KATYDID
15CM LONG (5.9 INCHES)

This Australian dry-leaf insect eats the leaves of the eucalyptus tree. It sits quietly on a twig like a dry leaf fluttering in the wind.

Its shape and color make it look exactly like a leaf. It is usually green, but there are also orange leaf insects that look like autumn leaves.

GIANT SPINY LEAF INSECT - 15CM LONG (5.9 INCHES)

There is always a dead leaf or two in the middle of all the green ones but there may also be one that is not dead at all! If you move closer, it suddenly opens up and you discover a beautiful butterfly. This is the Kalima, or Oakleaf Butterfly's strategy to confuse predators who have discovered it in spite of its camouflage.
The moment of surprise and indecision gives the butterfly a chance to fly away to safety.

When you live in the woods with predators all around, a good defense strategy is to hide or to make yourself look rather unappetizing! Millions of years of evolution have taught many insects how to do it better than anyone else can.

ORANGE OAKLEAF BUTTERFLY WINGSPAN 11CM (4.3 INCHES)

MASTERS OF CAMOUFLAGE

BEES OR WASPS?

It is easy to mix them up, but a close look shows that there are plenty of differences. To begin with, bees fly from one flower to another, taking the nectar from which they make honey, the sweetest food in the world. Wasps, on the other hand, are carnivorous and although some of them enjoy ripe fruit, they are the ones who try to steal the ham from our sandwiches during a picnic. If we look carefully, we can see that their stripes are black on a yellow background, not orange like the bees' stripes, and they have a narrower waist, what is known as a 'wasp waist'! Bees and wasps both have a poisonous stinger at the back tip of their bodies. Bees sting to defend themselves, but many wasps sting to kill other insects so that they can eat them or feed them to their larvae.

VIOLET CARPENTER BEE – 3CM LONG (1.1 INCHES)

It is often mistaken for a hornet, but in fact it is a bee and it is not aggressive; just leave it alone when it is flying around and looking for nectar!

ASIAN GIANT HORNET – 4.5CM LONG (1.7 INCHES)

Hornets build enormous, multi-storied nests with a very strong cardboard-colored covering that protects the cells. The colony of hornets uses the nest only for one year before they abandon it.

BUFF-TAILED BUMBLEBEE – 2CM LONG (0.7 INCHES)

Buff-Tailed Bumblebees (also known as Large Earth Bumblebees) are very hairy bees indeed! They build their nests in the ground and, like other bees, fly from flower to flower, looking for nectar.

EUROPEAN HONEY BEE – WORKER BEES 1.3CM LONG (0.5 INCHES); QUEEN BEE 2CM LONG (0.7 INCHES)

PAPER WASPS' NEST

PAPER WASP, 1.5CM LONG (0.5 INCHES)

Paper wasps build their
nests by making a past
of wood and saliva, to form
a sort of cardboard.
The cells are hexagonal and
contain the larvae that will
develop into adult wasps.
It is best to keep away from
their nests, because they
defend them very fiercely!

HONEYCOMB

Honeybees build large wax nests
known as honeycombs in the fissures
of old tree trunks, on rocks or
amongst the branches of the trees.
If we give them a home in a wooden
beehive, they will certainly make
a nest and produce delicious honey
for us every year!

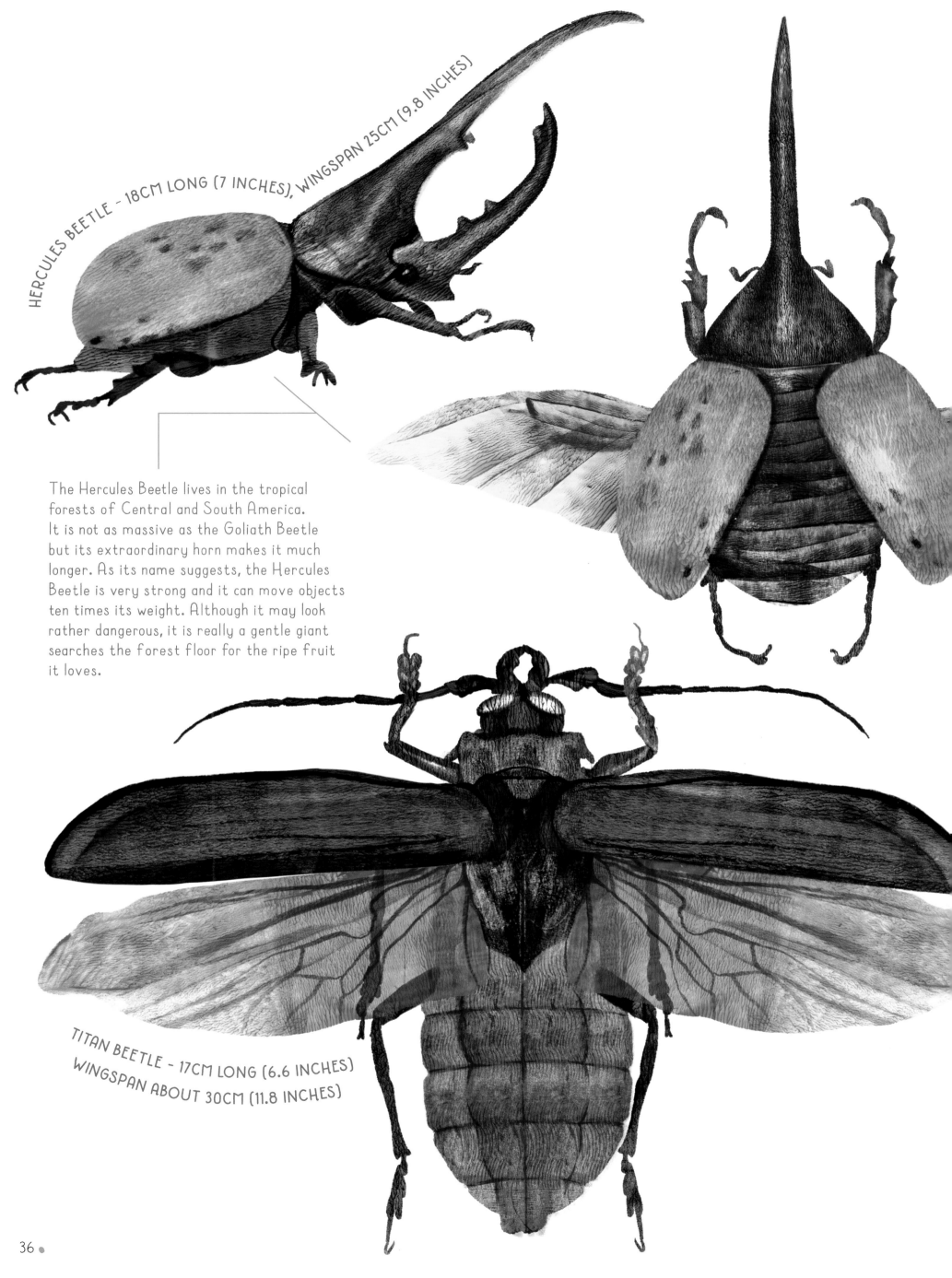

HERCULES BEETLE – 18CM LONG (7 INCHES), WINGSPAN 25CM (9.8 INCHES)

The Hercules Beetle lives in the tropical forests of Central and South America. It is not as massive as the Goliath Beetle but its extraordinary horn makes it much longer. As its name suggests, the Hercules Beetle is very strong and it can move objects ten times its weight. Although it may look rather dangerous, it is really a gentle giant searches the forest floor for the ripe fruit it loves.

TITAN BEETLE – 17CM LONG (6.6 INCHES)
WINGSPAN ABOUT 30CM (11.8 INCHES)

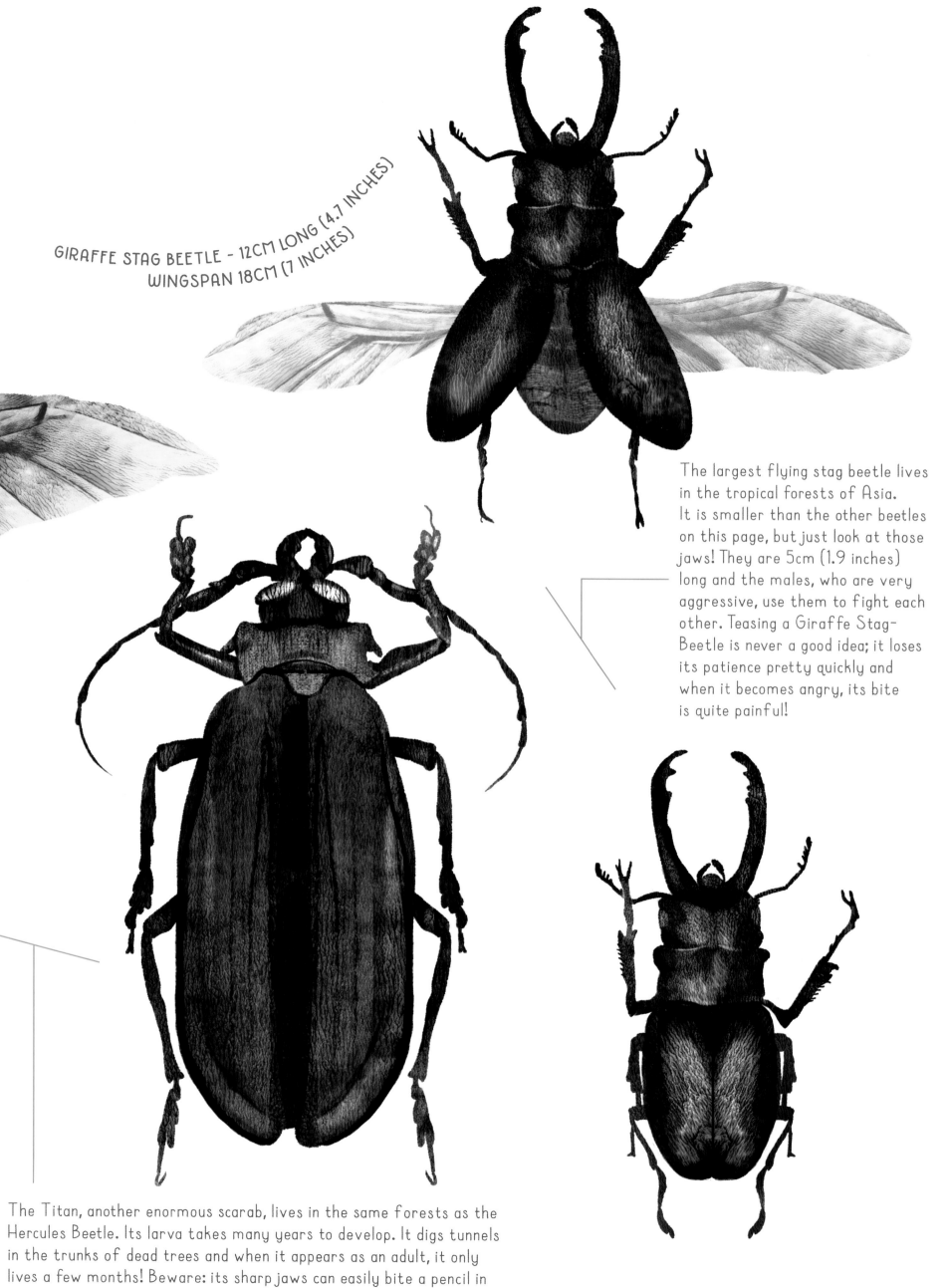

GIRAFFE STAG BEETLE - 12CM LONG (4.7 INCHES)
WINGSPAN 18CM (7 INCHES)

The largest flying stag beetle lives in the tropical forests of Asia. It is smaller than the other beetles on this page, but just look at those jaws! They are 5cm (1.9 inches) long and the males, who are very aggressive, use them to fight each other. Teasing a Giraffe Stag-Beetle is never a good idea; it loses its patience pretty quickly and when it becomes angry, its bite is quite painful!

The Titan, another enormous scarab, lives in the same forests as the Hercules Beetle. Its larva takes many years to develop. It digs tunnels in the trunks of dead trees and when it appears as an adult, it only lives a few months! Beware: its sharp jaws can easily bite a pencil in half so you are better off to leave it alone!

OH! THAT HURT!

If this young Velvet Monkey could speak, it would tell you that the Goliath Beetle neither bites nor stings, but that it is very strong! If you pick it up and your fingers accidentally end up in the spaces between its elytra, it might pinch you as it moves... and that would be very painful! Although it is not the longest beetle in the world, the Goliath beetle is the largest and heaviest. It lives in the African forests and flies from one tree to another, looking for its favorite food – sweet ripe fruit.

ROYAL GOLIATH BEETLE
11CM LONG (4.3 INCHES)

ISABELLA GROTT

Born in Rovereto in 1985, she graduated
from the Istituto d'Arte in Trento.
She then moved to Florence, where she
earned a degree in decorative arts at
the Accademia di Belle Arti (2007)
and a degree from the Accademia delle
Arti Digitali Nemo (2010). She then
began working in the world of children's
publishing, collaborating with a number
of publishing houses. She lives in
Florence with her inseparable cat
Miss Murple, where she works as
a freelance illustrator and teaches
at the Nemo Academy.

VALTER FOGATO

He is one of ADMaiora's most
important consultants – publicist,
graphic designer, illustrator and author
of popular science works and much more.
He has designed and set up numerous
dioramas for museums and visitor
centers at natural parks, also writing
the texts for the illustrative panels.
In particular, he created all the dioramas
for the world environments at the
Museo di Storia Naturale in Milan.

WSkids
WHITE STAR KIDS
White Star Kids® is a registered trademark property of White Star s.r.l.

© 2019 White Star s.r.l.
Piazzale Luigi Cadorna, 6
20123 Milan, Italy
www.whitestar.it

Translation: Iceigeo, Milan (Katherine M. Clifton, Cynthia Anne Koeppe)

ISBN 978-88-544-1343-6
 2 3 4 5 6   24 23 22 21 20

Printed in China

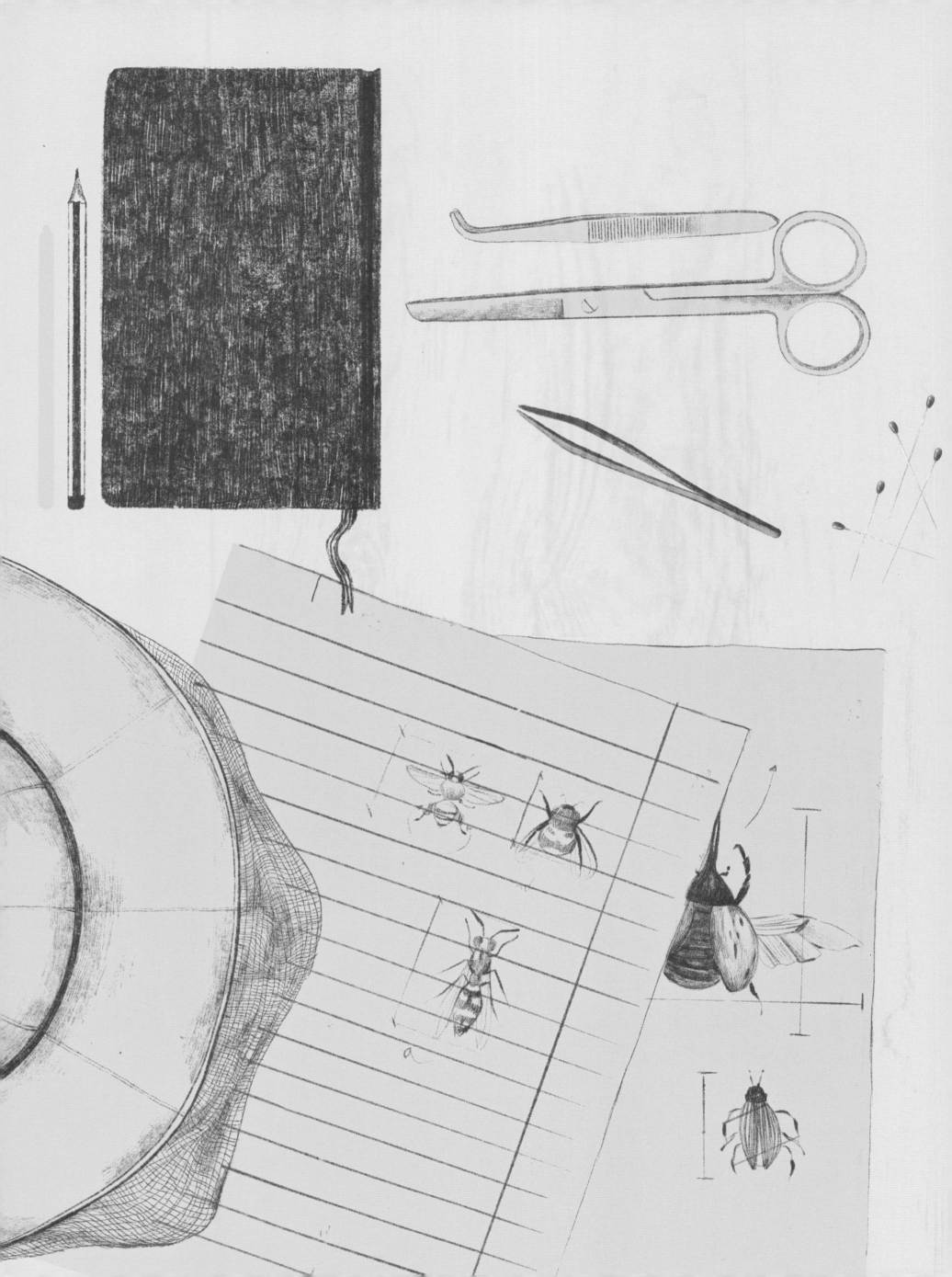